Waymakers

Eyewitnesses to the Christ

Sister M. Pamela Smith, SS. C. M.

AVE MARIA PRESS   Notre Dame, Indiana

International Standard Book Number: 0-87793-254-9

Library of Congress Catalog Card Number: 82-71664

Printed and bound in the United States of America.

Book design and illustration: Elizabeth French

CONTENTS

PART I: *The Messiah*

PART II: *The Passion*

PART III: *The Resurrection*

ACKNOWLEDGMENTS

Several of the poems included in this collection have appeared previously in theological or religious journals. The editors who have graciously given permission for their use in this book have my deep gratitude for their kindness and support.

The following poems are included herein with permission:

"The Annunciation," from the October 1975 issue of *Theology Today*, and "Peter, to His Knees," from the July 1975 issue of the same journal;

"Words From a Samaritan Woman" (under a slightly different title), from the February 1976 issue of *Sisters Today*;

"The Crosswalk" (spoken by Simon of Cyrene), accepted for use in *Contemplative Review*.

I am thankful also to a number of editors of various literary and religious magazines who have been accepting my work over the last 15 years. This present effort, my first book-length collection to be published, would not have come into being if it had not been for the interest and the imagination of Frank Cunningham, the editor of Ave Maria Press, whose vision transformed and unified this collection of poems on the experience of Christ.

For the work of assembling this collection, I have had the confidence and faith of Mother M. Raymund, Superior General of the Sisters of Saints Cyril and Methodius. She helped me initiate this project and then follow it through. I also have had the invaluable aid of Rev. Stephen Martin, C.S.B., Rev. Edward Heidt, C.S.B., and Rev. Gerald Sroka, Vicar for Religious for the Diocese of Gary, Indiana. All three took time to give my work a painstaking reading and to respond to the ideas and images contained in many of the poems, offering suggestions which helped this work while it was in progress. I shall always treasure in a very special way the wholehearted affirmation of the Sisters in my community and of our past Superior General, Mother M. Valeria. My impulse to write and to share what I write has received much encouragement from their interest and their willingness to serve as proofreaders and reactors to much of what I have written. I am grateful to my community, to my family, to my former teachers, and to my friends for the many ways in which they have enriched my life, helped me to love and create, and shown me the very-much-alive Christ.

Sister M. Pamela Smith, SS.C.M.

PART I

The Messiah

THE ANNUNCIATION

The moonglow in a manshape
after a light rain,
crooks and staffs
or the limbs of trees
tricking their shadows into angel wings,
the bleat of sheep on a far-off hill,
and the whistle of a stiff night wind—
perhaps it was nothing
but that on my pallet I had drowsed into a dream.

Yet the next morning I would have sworn
that there had been a man
or the ghost of a man
who announced himself as Gabriel
and hailed me "full of grace,"
yes, hailed, as if I were a princess,
a queen, a Roman empress, I . . . .

Perhaps it was nothing
but that on my pallet I had drowsed into a dream,
yet he foretold that I would bear a son,
a son whose name would be Emmanuel,
and I, a simple Hebrew girl, believed
but wondered how,
for there had never been a man . . . .
Perhaps it was nothing
but that on my pallet I had drowsed into a dream
and had awakened only now,
thinking that in my sleep
the power of the Most High God had overshadowed me
and come as the wings of a dove,
thinking that in my sleep
no man but a ghost called Gabriel . . . .

The moonglow in a manshape
after a light rain,
crooks or staffs
or the limbs of trees
tricking their shadows into angel wings,
and a ghost called Gabriel prophesying,
"And the Lord God will give him the throne of David his
    father,
and he shall be king over the house of Jacob forever"—
perhaps it was nothing
but the bleat of sheep on a far-off hill
and the whistle of a stiff night wind.

Luke 1:26-38

THE NIGHTWATCH

The Shepherds:

As the damp deepened
and the dark settled on the hills like dew,
as the sheep shifted in their sleep
and the stones softened
into shadow and wisp, we drew

our blankets around us and traded tales,
as if the stories we'd already told
a dozen times or more could keep
us watchful: manly rails
and wolf-safe gates about the fold.

Not danger exactly, but a terrible dazzling
came over us like a golden noonlight mist,
we just-snuggling herders and our sheep;
and the strange strains of hosannas, the razzle
of lyres, trumpets, manwomanchild-ranging voices, all
   bodiless,

drew us—sacredly, awestruck—to Bethlehem, to a barn,
to a boy about whom something, some look, some too-
   knowing embracing,
started such a leap

of fear and hope and beauty that in me no newborn,
not even of my own, could ever imprompt, ever upspring.

He is, he must be, the child of a long-ago promise, I believe.

My wife chides that I make too much of this baby,
that I have always seen things,
that when we pass the wineskins I weep
and make flat jokes, see by twos and threes, am moody,
am the butt of tricks, and hug and kiss and sing.

But since then this guard against wolves and thieves,
this shepherd who fears wrongdoing as if it were death, is
    relieved
that among the children of Israel the angel-hailed—and dare
    I say?—God-with-us sleeps.

Luke 2:8-20

ASTROLOGY

For myself, I have never known
what the stars might tell of love and justice.
That they seem to shape and display I can say,
and sometimes, for us skywatchers, they portend.
But what sane man, I ask myself, puts faith
in such wanton playthings as these sparkles of night?
What man of good sense rides camelback for hundreds of
    miles
because of some sign he suspects in the way the stars align?
And what wise man (and if I were he, wouldn't I know?)
stops his journey at a ramshackle shed
just because of a certain brightness, a certain cast of starlight,
kneels down, thinking of some hints in an ancient tome,
and worships, hoping that an age of illumination might
    begin?
What man bows to
—and feels blessed by—
an utterly ordinary baby boy?

Matthew 2:1-12

ANNA AND SIMEON TO THE YOUNG MOTHER

The Old Widow: When you have tallied up
as many years as we . . .

The Aged Priest: Seven swords at least
will have punctured your hopes,
your happiness,
your passion for your people
and the promises of the patriarchs.

The Old Widow: But you will live, not shuffling,
not childless,
not simply patient in your prayers
but signless,
not doddering into the afterworld as we . . .

The Aged Priest: No, you will last to see our people freed,
the dry bones of Ezekiel's field
slapped joyously to life,
and the strangest turnabouts of love, hate,
forgiveness, sin,
of death and birth,
serenity and strife.

The Old Widow: Mother of the Messiah,
the pain and splendor of centuries
lies helpless in your arms.

The Aged Priest: He who dismisses us
empowers you.

Together: Be peace.
Shalom.

Luke 2:22-40

15

THE CARPENTER OF NAZARETH

Joseph:

The woman,
the woman I could never hold to
but have clasped forever, it seems, soul to soul;
the son who could never belong to me,
the boychild with his cryptic answers, his enigmas, his
   perceptions, his everything astonishing,
the son who could never belong to anyone but One,
the man who no longer, at twelve, feels altogether at
   home . . . .

Over my sawhorse I muse,
over my carpenter's tools . . .
the house of David,
this house in Nazareth,

"My Father's house,"
"My Father's business" . . . .
Which is building.
(Though none would ever dream of angels and ancient texts
or imagine what any of them have to do with this.)
Building.

Someday they will surely say,
"Isn't this the carpenter's son?"
Merely . . . .
"Isn't . . . ?"
This boy who is expert in woodgrains and weights,
who fondles what he turns and hammers,
this boy who is an artist and tradesman
already, himself.
"Isn't this the carpenter's son?"
Unnoticed, I will insinuate that there is something
    undisclosed.
More secret than the secrets of my father and his and his
and the whole family line,
confided when a man grasps his firstborn around the neck
and blesses him . . . .
Secrets of a craft and generations and faith . . . .
Mary . . . .
The firstborn . . . .
To consecrate and foster but never to father at all.
My wife, the maid
who is a masterpiece of love and grace . . . .
Both of us, the three of us, a bit against the grain.

And waiting, aging.
You might say that my life,
like the form that wakes from the worker's wood,
has been a keeping still and trusting
another hand to cut and lathe, sand and shape.
O Maker, O Master,
O Adonai of David,
O one who duped and used
and fashioned and smoothed the prophets,
O Mystery who has made of my dead wood
a green, an infinitely flowering Tree,
I praise, I hold to, Thee.

Matthew 1:18-25, 2:13-15
Luke 2:41-52

THE COUSIN

John the Baptist:

It was when the water cascaded
through his hair and down his face
that the words crashed through, a shiver, a cloudbreak.
". . . My beloved son. Listen to him."

When we were tykes playing in the sand,
and later, when we were ten or eleven,
we imagined palace houses, adventure,
tales of the East, ladders to heaven.

He said once that he would be a wise man,
and I pictured him on a camel, turbanned.
I thought I would serve in the temple, like Zechariah,
but I dreamed of digging out the ark or Eden.

That was before the wild skins and the tan
of searing weather and stark wilderness—
before I forefasted, before I foreran,
before the unrolling of the scroll of the plan

that is his Father's.
          The voice which spoke this morn
was one I detected in the forlorn
night cry of the desert. I have heard it
before—before, it almost seems, I was born.

Matthew 3:1-17

ANDREW

I will admit to being excitable—
as impetuous perhaps as my brother—
and an exhorter, almost a politician,
in the way I catch a cause, the tempo of the times,
and mention this, then that, about him—
as a winsome man with a new idea or two
gathers momentum, draws one mob after another, and
    becomes a movement.
First it was the Baptizer, then the teacher he nicknamed—
peculiarly, it seemed to me—the Lamb.
But if I had really understood what was rippling across
    the land,
rippling as the thrown stone wakes waves in the lake,
or, better yet, as the angel stirs the pool at Bethesda and
    sickness fall away,
I would not just have collared Simon
and hauled him off to meet him
swearing, "Brother, this is the One. This is finally the Messiah."
No, I would have bellowed from Galilee to Judaea;
I would have climbed Sinai and come down with fire in my
    eyes;
I would have blown the most resonant ram's horn I could
    find
and blown it from sunup till dusk and from dusk again till
    dawnlight;
I would have bullied the fisherfolk, the herdsmen,
    the farmers,

taken the women charmingly by the arm,
pushed the crippled, the ill, the old ones, in wheelbarrows,
tugged the children along, perching the littlest on my
    shoulders,
delighted all the while as they squirmed or poked my eyes or
    yanked my hair;
I would have kissed on both cheeks every man who jeered
    at me,
and I'd have squatted at the city gates with the beggars,
raved like a lunatic or gone in for the dramatics of a
    Jeremiah
if that would have won them to him.
But I had just begun to guess.
I did not yet have that flood of zeal and love.
Not yet.

John 1:35-42

NATHANAEL

I was only a man who daydreamed
and would have wished to forget a few things.
A plump fig, I sat there under the leaves,
ripe for picking.
If only I had known he could mindread . . . .

John 1:43-50

MATTHEW LEAVES HIS
TAX TABLES

The question, finally, was one of treasures
and what to do about moths and rust.

Matthew 6:19-21, 9:9-13

PETER, TO HIS KNEES

Because I can't
                              (Depart from me, O Lord)
tug in the loaded fishnets
or skim across Gennesaret

                              (for·I am a sinful man)
—the network rips apart
and water washes over my knees, my thighs, above my waist,
   my chest,
water washes up to my neck . . . .

Because after we yank and heave in our catch
the skiff goes deadweight and begins to sink
and after I take a few breezy steps
I halt leadfooted when a sudden gust grabs my breath . . . .

                         (If it is you)
Dragging, drowning,
head, hands, feet . . .
and the nets—tangles and snapping frets—
and the waves—their storming crests and troughs . . . .
I am afraid
of the lake bottom and a headwind.

Because you rock my heart . . . .

                         (Lord, order me to come)
Because I can't,
though you are just a quick cast out into the deep
or a stone's throw away . . . .
Because I can't,
I pray.

Matthew 14:22-33

THE LAST DAY OF THE HEMORRHAGE

A touch, like the tenderest tap of a fond friend,
a quick grab, like the catching at the first skirt by a tiny
   lost child,
that was all. Then a tingle,
and the searing stopped and the blood dried.
I am shy of whatever struck me from his body,
and I still can't fathom his manner of medicine,
his oceanic eyes that seemed to pour into the core of me,
and the so much compassion that spoke from him, reticent.

Mark 5:25-34

THE CENTURION TO WHOSE HOUSE HE DIDN'T COME

If I'm not mistaken, he seemed a bit amused.
We great men know all about commands, I remarked,
as if I were cozying up with the leaders of cohorts
or sealing a confidence with another toughened, brusk
   authority.

All I was worrying about, really, was that servant boy,
and, wanting him well, I'd have tried any miracleworker or
   messiah.
Great faith? Well, that has come more of late.
That day I caught the twinkle. "We great men," I'd said.

The healer made it easy, almost silly,
as if the servant had his sympathy already.
He asked; he commanded nothing; and he knew
   it was done.
His smile said that great men give over all things to their God.

Luke 7:1-10

NICODEMUS

A fraidy-cat in spite of my Pharisee propriety, my pomp,
a sucker for esteem among the Sanhedrin, and wanting only
    good gossip,
I slunk like a stealthy prowler to see him by night.
It was, if it matters, a Wednesday.

Wrapped in my solitude as in the prayer shawl,
weeks later, I keep trying to decipher it.
If only I could read him
as one pores over the lines of the law . . .

I still do not understand about the water.
I wonder about the wind.
How to be born again? In what womb?
I wrack these runes like a myopic scribe.

In the terrors of my sleep,
when I am drowning,
when the wind blows me away,
when I cannot gulp a breath of air
or catch hold of the limb of a tree,
it is always he who rescues me.

John 3:1-21

TESTIMONY OF A DEMONIAC

Rats scurried across and scratched about the prison that was
   my mind,
and the night bats swooped low, beating across my brow.
Weeds grew from the grime beneath my toenails
   and between my toes
while my fingers turned to claws and snakes sizzled
   under my skin,
and whenever I giggled lightning shredded leaves, split trees,
   rolled rocks and scree down cliffs,
and my words were leprous froth.

"Enough!" he ordered when I catcalled his name,
"Jesus of Nazareth."
And the tombstones of my soul cracked open.
That was this morning, another life ago.

I am noticing, as for the first time,
the soft blue of the sky,
the green slopes and the undersides of leaves,
the chittering of insects and the grace of birds,
the smoothness, the light strength of women's hands,
laughter,
the savor of bread;
and, as the day cools to dusk,
I think fondly of the villager's house,
the welcome fire, lightly spiced wine;
I warm at the hum of men's shoptalk and chortling,
the candledancing breezes,
the excellence and wonder of childsong.

"Son of the All Holy," I called him—
or, rather, the foreign voice within me. Why?
I look forward to a good night's sleep.
Then I must tell them all back home.
I shall tell them all at home:
Yes, it is I.

Luke 8:26-39

THE LEPER

If I could begin to tell you what it is like
to have watched yourself rot and ooze away for years,
you might begin to see how amazed, how wild
with glee, how crazed we were to be—suddenly!—clean.
You'd know why most rushed headlong, nonstop, to the
   priests.
You'd know why a few paused, turning this way, then that,
   lost,
foreign to their own hands and feet, dazed into helplessness.

When I raced back to fall on my knees, to pour
out my wonder upon him, and even to adore
this one who seemed a god in the flesh, he did not
seem to object to this fraction of gratefulness.
                               When
he asked after the other nine, it was not as a man
who'd been disappointed at something—but more like
an old friend who seeks news of those he hasn't seen for a time.

Luke 17:11-19

31

EPHPHATHA: BE OPEN

My world, like everyone's, was overlaid
with barriers, blockades,
a muffled, tongue-tied world
where speech fails and voices fade
into buzz or hum or the silences of stone.
My world, like everyone's, had withdrawn. Alone,
I cared so little for myself, for anyone,
I conjectured that I'd have nothing to say
if one should come who could break the blocks, hurl
the walls across my senses down. Girls,
boys, women, men, my kin—
uncanny—carried me to him.
I cared little. My world, like everyone's,
was fingers in the ears, loose spit on the tongue.
Then he spoke a word. And all my world fell away.

Mark 7:31-37

WORDS FROM A SAMARITAN WOMAN

The breeze, the blessed breeze,
the merest waft of wind,
the health of sun on my back,
a long, luxurious draft of water
and a quiet place to sit—
these (oh woman, I swear,
though five husbands could not slake your thirst,
and your jars empty out,
and you keep trudging back)
these, I swear, are more than enough,
for I, weakened and bone-dry,
know that out of nowhere—
out of do-dads in the dust—
a whole heaven suddenly wells up.

John 4:4-30, 39-42

THE UNBLINDING

What I have seen today
I could never have seen with my eyes anyway.
Nothing that is mere man,
nothing that looks like trees;
I have seen spirit, awakening,
the future in the making, liberty.
Though I gaze and now know
that the sun is yellow, the sky blue,
that his eyes are even warmer
than the voice I felt to my fingertips,
to the startlement of my heart,
I have seen beyond all looking.
I have seen a prophet who sees through me.
I have been unblinded frighteningly,
and I welcome it—revel, rejoice—
yet dread that I am on the edge of terror and mystery;
for I sense he is the undoing of all that I was.
I have seen the breaking in half of history.

Mark 8:22-26

THE ADULTERESS,
AFTER HE DOODLED
IN THE STREET

As one scoops up sand and, slowly, opening the fist
and separating, stretching fingers, lets it sift
until upon the spread palm
only a few grey, a few glassy, grains are left,
and those one can wistfully blow away:
so he parted me from my last lover, my past,
my captors, my sins, my dread of death,
my sorry image of God, my expectation of wrath.

John 8:2-11

A NEIGHBOR FROM NAZARETH

Maybe the fact that he couldn't come through
with any stupendous signs back here
proves that he's not much of anyone.
But I'm still rather taken aback
by that Isaiah scroll moment.
And there is all that talk from Capernaum,
those rumors, really, across the whole countryside.
He was always a good boy.
I can't imagine him just going off
and saying such unheard of things and doing stunts.

Mark 6:1-6
Luke 4:16-30

BARLEY LOAVES AND FISH

I have cried wolf and have told fish stories,
so of course they didn't believe this one.
My mother called me a thief, a wicked snippet,
when I brought home just a couple of the filled baskets.
I tried to tell them about the hungry thousands and about Jesus.
My mother's sisters all agree I am a prevaricator and a
  pickpocket
like my disappeared father. They say I inherited it.

John 6:1-13

ZACK

"Buddy, I'll be coming home with you—
if I'm welcome, I mean." That from Jesus,
after I'd just scrambled up the tree
to see over soldiers' helmets, children on shoulders,
and the high heads of Pharisees and priests.
That, after I near-missed tumbling into
the lap of a fat woman whose legs gave out
in the close crowd, the hot pressing, and the market stink.
Worse yet, after he shot a look into the treetops,
almost as if, you know, he didn't mean to,
I blubbered up that list of wonderful things,
which, of course, were all about me.

"Zacchaeus, hurry down."
                              But since that night
it has been nothing but up, mitzvah, for me.
No one, I swear, can sit and talk, can eat
and laugh, can pray and speculate with that man
without becoming tall, wise, loving, smart—
altogether—I can't explain—more than he was when He was not.

Luke 19:1-10

JOANNA'S PENCE

My husband Chuza keeps Herod fat-fed
and puffed up, and, for all I know,
may have garnished the Baptizer's head
on the platter for the laughter, the throes
of smiling spite, of Salome and her mother.
Chuza the steward is a sycophant, a pleaser.
I would be nauseous of one party after another,
if I were he.
                    His wife, his lover: I am neither.

For the years I lazed, perfumed and silk-clad,
stone-blind as the bat by day
to the orphan, the lazar, the ragtag,
I repent. I use dear Chuza's ill-got pay
to grub together bread, a room
where thirteen men can lay their road-wrung bones,
a sleeve patch, a sandal thong, whatever boon
the Galilean needs.
                    For I am one he owns.

Luke 8:1-3

JAMES ON TABOR

I can tell you only the words of my body.

I went prostrate,
for a voice rumbled up
from the circle of cloud
and called him "Son"
and enjoined us to listen.

I lay flat.
I lay still.
I heard, with his,
our three hearts beating
and the mountain moving slightly
with our breathing.

Soundless, I prayed.
Until he touched us,
I could have crushed, slowly,
into the earth,
softened by a mist of rain.
For hundreds of days, till he touched us,
I could have stayed and stayed and stayed.

Matthew 17:1-8

MARTHA: EVERYBODY'S FAVORITE FUSSBUDGET SAINT

I wouldn't call my sister loose, but laid back.
She listens.
She never thinks to lift a lid or test a roast or wipe a
  dish clean.
She is in love with a Jewish hero.
She memorizes scrolls of Isaiah.
She talks of a new law.
She sits.
I would swirl like a sirocco and swear at her
if it were not that I have been gentled
by this itinerant rabbi who likes to rest in Bethany,
by his friends with their ideals and visions
(like Peter's mother-in-law,
I'm always wanting to fatten them),
by my own sister who swallows the Master's words whole
and, I hate to say it, is transparent—
and nearly as swept away as Elijah.
Sometimes I think the entire covey of disciples
could forget for days to eat, to sleep,
to do anything common-sensed and ordinary.
But, as surely as I know seasonings, slow cookery, and the
  art of timing,
I see that a day of the Lord is upon us
and that maddening Mary is impeccably, holily sane.
As for the rest, perhaps like Moses they—

and I too, for I am turning their way—
speak with God face-to-face . . .
and, doing that, must lose or forget some semblances of the
   everyday.

Luke 10:38-42

AMBITION:
FROM THE MOTHER OF JAMES
AND JOHN

The hardest was the part about their drinking the cup,
not that we understood it,
for his words broke over us
and left a wake of anger among the others.
It was just that I felt Zebedee's sons
noble enough for some assurance.
But what are they to quaff?
And what of his solemn remarks—as if
he wished to flood us not with wonder this time
but with warning and puzzlement—
what of his cryptic remarks about their being servants?
James and John were not raised to be table waiters,
but, of course, that can't be what he meant.
He meant, I think, that there is something they will not
   merely drink;
there is something in which they will be drenched.

Matthew 20:20-28

A WIDOW OF NAIM

At best, I have middle-aged and mediocred—
suffered the death of love before I was an actual widow,
slopped my talk with gossip,
and slackened and slothed about what used to be
crisp meals and a well-kept house.
And I have been casual with God,
circling around the sabbaths with distractions and smalltalk
   and long snoozes—
just as one who is at odds with a father winds the longest
   way home from the well,
pausing to pet animals, to gawk at every market stall,
zigging and zagging up all the alleys of the village and down.
I have prayed—which is to say not much at all,
just as I tend to be sparse with endearments and
   tendernesses—
with little fervor and less faith,
unable to imagine either a thunderer on Sinai
or Elijah's gentle breeze.

When my son died, I was so used to unfeeling,
to old losses and long silences and the lengthening numbness
   of my soul,
that I could not complain or sob onto someone's shoulder or
   recall one psalm as a whole.
And so there could have been no one more mystified than I
when this rabbi or prophet or comeback Elijah raised him.
He was merely passing by.

I remember no one who ever begged a cup of water, a bite of
    bread,
a slice of oil-and-flour cake from me
and met extravagant generosity.
No, I have been a dried up fig, exquisitely stingy.

My son was—he is again or still, I should say—a promising
    youth,
no thanks due myself; but this holy man seemed to favor not
    him but me.
To hear some of the neighbor ladies, you'd think I was the
    beloved of God,
as if for years I'd kept the precious secret of my sanctity
like a treasure or a jewel under cover in a crock or cached in
    a hollowed-out chunk of the house.
You'd think, the way they've questioned me, that I've had
visitations of angels and have lodged and fed visionaries
    regularly.
But I know little of this Jesus and less of what he might want
    with me.
My son barely speaks of him but says that he has touched
    the All-Holy.

If the Nazarene is really what a few of the pious whisper him
    to be,
he is the son of Someone who has loved me no matter what
and known that my son was the last, the sole, warm wind
that could waft across my heart.

Luke 7:11-17

LITTLE GIRL, GET UP

"Talitha, koum."
From dreamripe sleep,
from the magic springtime
of wheeling water
and blossomed clouds,
from phantasms of flowers
and fields of toys
and ruddy children
running the sunshine in armloads
to brighten the faces of parents and old folks,
from color and cavorting,
the healer called me.
At his foreign-tinted words,
from the most May-like morning,
I came home or maybe I awoke
from a playland faraway.

I can't remember any more exactly,
and the difference between where I was
and where I am I can't explain.
He was a nice man,
and I felt I had met him out there,
before he hailed me alive or awake.
I think he said it would be kinder later—
the fruit trees, the oasis wet and warm, the games—
and that there would be angels and everyone I'd love.
I felt a dew like summer sabbaths
left on my fingers, my face.

Mark 5:21-24, 35-43

LAZARUS

Having come forth once, my Lord, my Friend,
I await my second death
like a man who warms, smiles, whistles a little
as he wends his way,
after vagabond months and years of days,
to his loves, to his kin, to the lifebread of home.

John 11:1-44

THE MITE OF MONEY

It wasn't anything,
though the one watching remarked on it to his hangers-on.

Poor, plain-faced, pitying almost everyone
because I have no pity left for myself,
I have become a parable.

I pray to the God who imagined Isaac,
the God of laughter.

Notice, O disciples,
it really was nothing.
Nor are my purse, my pockets.
Nor is my widowhood.
Nor is the temple.

God is, which is enough.

Mark 12:41-44

PART II

The Passion

PHILIP

We were moments away from the breaking, the blessing,
the passing of wine in the cup from gloss to Godliness,
the turning of the whole world
—every old thought, every expectation,
every sense of what *was* from Sheol to third heaven—
inside out, totally around, upside down, wild and
   contrariwise,
when I blundered.
                    The schlemiel. The schnook. I
asked him to show me what I was looking at but had never
   seen.
I asked him to take me where I already was.
If it had been I, my patience would have been more than
   strained.
I would have walked off exasperated,
feeling as if I had just wasted months explaining myself

to a man with the mind of a lizard.
He was tired. He seemed vaguely puzzled, incredulous,
 pained.
And so he began again, as if it were his last earthly chance.

John 14:8-11

AUGURY: WHAT IS TRUTH?

Pilate:

I lay waiting for the inside of an answer,
a configuration of vowels and consonants,
the entrails of animals winding into a word,
into words, into words, words, words,
into an augury,
into a side-splitting joke,
into a sentence, yes,
a sentence of death.

John 18:33-38

THE CROSS, TAKEN

A Bystander:

When you can free-fall into the black holes in the hill trees
without looking for shade or nest space
and follow the butterflies past the clover where they
  dipsy-doodle and disappear,
when you can rest amid a blizzard of bees,
plumb the zero of cocoon and honey comb
without a thought of what or how to eat,
and tread sweating from the noon heat into a cold midnight
  of a skull heap,
then you will know, I think.

I watched him shoulder the crossbeam
and have not been able to rock to sleep.

John 19:16-17

ONE DOWNFALL

A Sick Woman From the East:

Gripped in the clock-tick of good days and bad days,
juggled upside down and rightside up between strong surges
   and weak spells,
I know what it is to be tugged to the sunset,
to wish and wish that somewhere over, somewhere ever . . . .
I know what it is to crush from inside out and slither
   into a hole.

Today and ever after a man slapped to the ground.
And, curlicue, curlicue, something is new,
I'm charmed like a snake to a Hindu flute.
I gather up strength and self and—God!—
I do and do and do.

Isaiah 53:3-5

THE MEETING OF MOTHER AND SON

A 'Friend of His Mother:

This evening (in the wing-furl, nicely off left behind my ear,
in the wind-weave of a widow-wept cypress tree)
the gaggle of day fades
into a kind of make-believe,
the bad dream from which one wakes with a knot in the
    stomach
and slowly eases up, unties, with the waking eye's relief.

I don't understand
(but the breeze and a way off blather of birds)
the wind boil of scourge and drag, cross-walk, thorns, nails,
    vinegar, and a terrible outcry
that sinks into a sickness, then a sigh.

The gaggle of the day fades
(with a wing-furl of blackbirds and the wind-weave in a
    cypress tree),
but, oh, I remember his face.
as the Sabbath dusks and dawns and breaks,
oh, yes, I remember, I remember his face.

Wisdom 3:1-9
1 Corinthians 1:18-21

THE CROSSWALK

Simon of Cyrene:

Hubbubbed, in the muddle of the cutthroats,
they juggled me as if I were a thug
and crushed me to this Jesus
lugging his own deadwood up,
this Jesus who had dropped.
Beside myself, against their fisticuffs,
mad as the buzz of spittle in the mud,
I heaved the crossbar up from him and tugged.

We walked.

Little by little, as I felt his breath on my neck,
felt his sweat,
I worried for this knockabout they mocked.
There had been a story about him doodling in the dust
when they went to stone a floozy.
He loved her up.
Slowly, like the crank-turn on a half-stuck, rusted water well,
my rage quelled, and the cross seemed almost weightless.

Huddling it for him was not too much.

Mark 15:21

THE FACECLOTH

Veronica:

On the sort of morning when the chutes of sunlight through
    the trees
summerstruck the grassblades, the weedmats, the pods,
    and stunned the soil itself,
it was hard to think of anything so large as the face of
    God—
with this all-so-much-enough of dewdrop, insect buzz,
    and birdsong.

But I saw him—amid the overhaul of paradisaical morning to
    a God-forsaken afternoon,
that Friday which upturned the walkway to deaddust,
brush skudding across a desert, and the sky a stinkpot,
all aswirl, then stockstillness
(the cattle unchewing, uncudding, huddling; the horses, all
    ear-alert, unmunching)
to, later, the earthquake.

His was a pain-face, bruised, filthy with sweat and skin-oil,
    whiskered, blood-splotched.
With a swipe, when I rushed him from the mob, in a love spasm,
    I saw and swept him with my veil.
He was thin, and I expected nothing of him,
much less this relic.

I didn't know him from Adam.
Yet now I must tell what no headcloth/facecloth ever will:
through the shadows roundabout his eyes,
with the day darkening like a tempest mid-sea and a rumble
    starting to roll underfoot,
from the black dead-center hideaway of his eyes, his eyes,
broke such devastating and unearthly flares of dawnlight.

Matthew 5:7-8

THE SECOND COLLAPSE

A Roman Soldier:

I only began to poke at him,
and it was as if my pike were a magic lever
or a slow-motion catapult.

Something groaned in him,
and I felt a cord of wind wrap tight around my neck,
drawing my breath, my heaving chest, my arms to a halt
as he scuffled with the soil itself
and rose, almighty stubborn, up.

Isaiah 50:5-8

JERUSALEM AWAKENING

One of the Met Women, after a Spell of Rough Days:

I have gone to bed these two nights
(a dull dragging down in me)
half-believing I might die.
This night.

Life is rich and wondrous in whatever I am, yes
—dazzled prayer-maker, mother, teacher, wife, cook,
   keeper of the house and guests—
and I treasure the love-laugh, the smile, the sullen child,
   the kin, the friend, the pest.
I treasure the gnarled apple boughs, the fire, and the fly.
The going to the ground.
I treasure death.

So, I believe I have begun to understand the fatigue
   of that Jesus,
the ache in the back of the head that revolves and veers
till it wheels around the face, then rises, narrows,
spins about the eyes, his eyes,
his eyes that half-saw and sickened at and pitied us women
   of Jerusalem,
the fatigue of that Jesus who died.
Rabbi, we women are wondrous, yes,

and even our wail, our bloodlet, our nursing infants
   are rich. But.
In dreaming my death I remember your words and wonder
   what we have missed.

I go for more.
And as I have weakened, I also am up again,
praising the lightening of my sick, stiff bones and cartilage,
the thinning of my thick and sticky blood,
the surge of muscle, the verve,
crying out to the mystery of which that Jesus, Rabbi, dead
   man, prophesied,
raising, as I rise, my arms to the God who fathered all of
   this.
This night.
Life is rich and wondrous in whatever I am—
a night dance.

Luke 23:27-31

THIRD FALL

A Pike Carrier:

He no longer slammed down hard but slithered.
He no longer groveled against the ground, stumbling up,
but lay *in* it, *with* it.
He licked it.

Now that he had completely collapsed,
the snake he was coiled and watched some old shadow,
some shed skin
(the peeling self that was sin),
wobble of itself, stand up, and carry on,
double-crossed.

Psalm 22:7-16
1 Peter 4:1-2

THE DISROBING

A Boy:

They tore him all away
as they'd yank burning clothes from a baby.
If I wake up in the middle of the night,
will I see anything besides blood and pus and ripped skin?
I am so afraid that I'll remember the naked man.
Were they trying to pull their hatred off him?

John 19:23-24

NAILED: THE TIME WARP

Jesus:

Outside of the body
(when almost everything shatters, as if tiny little icicles hang
    from your eyelashes and drip down to the sizzling tropic of
    your lower lid and then slide down your nose and your
    tongue detects a drop of sweat wondering where it can
    have come from)

Outside of the body
(when a thump somewhere ages down your arm reminds you
    of the shudder of Noah's ark on a mountaintop
    somewhere in Russia which of course no one has heard of
    yet and another thump apparently means the soldier or
    another soldier or anyone at all has rammed the other
    spike into your hand because at least that is how the story
    goes and you can't help but wondering how long it will be
    before they discover innermost Africa and the Titanic will
    strike an iceberg)

Or was it yesterday,
debris in a whirlpool,
this dumb daze,
and a voice (flooded-out and faraway) uttering (when?)
"Father, forgive them."

Mark 15:33-36
Luke 23:34

THE EVERLASTING MOMENT OF DEATH: CONSUMMATION

John:

My beloved.
(Now I shall call you that,
and I will carry your corpse in my arms
for as long as I can
and hold you through the sad wrapping
and place you like my brother, my father, my friend
on that cold stone.)
I wish you sleep,
I wish you more than the peace you promised to leave.
Though I understand maybe less than Philip,
I am here, and I shall never let loose
the moments when your magnificent love
warmed me like a home fire.
The bread is broken.
The cup is passed.
I may never touch your shoulder nor hear you laugh nor
   glimpse the sea in your eyes again,
yet, my beloved,
I am sure that this is not quite all,
not the very end.

John 19:26-27, 21:20-25

PIETA

Mary the Mother:

I cannot sob like the women at Ramah,
wail like Rachel for her chilren.
I cannot call out, "Absalom, my son, my son!"
though he is no more, and my heart weeps for the thorns,
  the nails, the cross.
I am not comforted in the arms of gentle, steady John,
and the curtain of the temple itself is torn.

The sword thrust into my side
has left no evident gaping wound,
has spilled no water, no blood,

but I am more than ever before
hurt—and mystified by His Father.
I mourn inwardly, waiting for,
wondering at—what?—
believing, utterly given in,
but speechless as Zechariah.

John 19:25-30

A ROCK-REST

Joseph of Arimathea:

The very least I could give him
was this last black hole
in which he could sink into himself,
float away (selah, selah), or explode.

Mark 15:42-46

PART III

The Resurrection

SUNDAY, IN THE CLEARING

Mary Magdalene:

I have known and I have been the wasted woman
who ranged the city aching, urging, fainting for her lover.
For me Solomon wrote no hymns.
But in this amazing Jesus I leapt to life
and poured myself out for him, like oil, like perfume,
and I, who lasted with no one—never!—stayed with him
along dustwalks and grassy hills and finally on that
   boneheap
till the midday sky blackened over and every breath caught,
   startled.

I have puttered around garden and tomb,
bundling and bearing flowers, ointments, fresh gravecloths,
distracting myself from the truth.
No, he could never be gone,

not this only one who penetrated me with his eyes, his mind
and held me dear as a planter who sees a flower, a
   wheatsheaf, a tree in the paltriest seed.
No, he could not disappear,
not this only one who ever fully knew me and (my God!)
   always smiled.

Perhaps my eyes will never be dry,
or perhaps this man who shades his eyes from the sun
will pause from his gazing at all the dumb green things that
   grow here
and tell me some one item, hint at where, with whom,
   why . . .

John 20:11-15

SEVENTY TIMES SEVEN

The Gardener:

"Mary!"

John 20:16-18

THEN, IN EMMAUS

He seemed, at first, a pure intelligence,
the walker with his face half masked
from the dust and heat.
His words washed over us
as we hastened into the haze,
late in the day.
A wise man he was, we nodded to one another—
a rahb of texts and explanations.
These things had to happen, he averred.
    (And I remembered the arrest among the olives,
    the skinny disciple who dropped his clothes
    and could have shed his skin with fear,
    the thorns and lashes,
    the mob,
    the face of Barabbas shocked utterly out of the familiar
      sneer,
    the weeping,
    the rage,
    our helpless dismay,

the earthquake,
the "Into Your hands,"
the immense silence,
then, "Papa, Papa.")

And though we had begun our walk nervous chatterboxes,
we were inside still stunned to nothingness,
but he awoke our wondering, our ancient faith.
    (And a curl of smoke sifted up
    from the ashes gasping their last
    under the ring of stones which was my soul,
    and I asked my so slowly kindling self
    if I had ever known life or God,
    if I had ever worshipped or loved blind.)

And by the time we came to Emmaus we were fire.

He seemed, then, more than heart or mind.
And I, for one, I Cleopas,
have never so prevailed upon a man
to stay, to be a guest, to eat.

    When he sundered bread,
    such light and flame broke over us
    that we, though speechless, must have shone.
    And cupped in the hands of the man
    ("Behold him," the procurator had said)
    we glimpsed more worlds than we had ever wanted,
    ever known.

Luke 24:13-35

THE SKEPTIC

There is a strangeness in every rustle at the house back
and a start in every stone that rolls off to the road edge—
as if someone were stealing in to surprise his long-lost kin
with every scuff in the street and click of the doorlatch,
as if the stones themselves could raise a song
from the kick and clatter of chariot wheels and mule-drawn
     carts.

I, Thomas, will never quite trust my senses again,
nor deem anything impossible,
nor say, with certainty, that a man is dead.
Eerily, he passes through walls, he speaks,
he takes a bite to eat; he is fresh flesh.
Meanwhile, I feel that the change in him has thrown
a whole house open in everyone;
that the earthsounds
echo harmonies I've just begun to detect;
that I, the absent, must continually confess
that an unseen universe edges the old one out.
And, as strangers knock and stones reel from the
     wheels of a cart,
I touch holes, I shove into, through, shadows. My Lord and my God.

John 20:24-29

MARY AWAITING PENTECOST

It descends,
the world-searer.
Hot.
And once again
I will be scorched.
Fiat.

Acts 1:12-14